On I & Time

ON I & TIME

*Am I an isolated mind
or is there a brain model to explain my consciousness?*

SOHEIL SOLHJOO

Staten House

© Soheil Solhjoo 2024
All rights reserved.

First edition
ISBN 979-8-89379-013-9 (hardcover)
ISBN 979-8-33802-160-6 (paperback*)

*The paperback edition is published by Soheil Solhjoo via Amazon Kindle Direct Publishing.

Published by Staten House

The **FREEDOM OF CHOICE** hasn't always been accessible, but if everyone who can contributes to its advancement, it will eventually become universally available.

Contents

The Garden of Life — vi

Preface — viii

Outline of the book — x

On I — 1
    The originality of the mind 3
    The originality of the body 10
        From unicellular to animal 13
        All is by chance 15
        The brain: a model 15
        The emergence of memory 17
        Adequacy of the brain model 25
        The impacts of the nested memory units 27
        Foundations of 'I' 30
    The origin, the creation 33

On I—Further discussions — 35
    Why language? 36
    The fictitious power of M3 40
    Phenomena 42

Supersition	43
Mirror self-recognition test	44
Sleep terror & lucid dream	45
Colonies & societies	46
Nature and Nurture	48
Brain damage	49

On Time — 53

A hypothetical world	54
Stand-still worlds	56
Worlds with moving objects	57
Defining DAY and HAND	59
Perception of time for a stationary observer	59
Perception of time for a moving observer	59
Comparing the observed timelines	60
Conclusions	63
The world before creation	64

On Time—Further discussions — 65

Our perception of time	66
Confusions in the perceived time	69
Short-term confusions	69
Long-term confusions	73
The possibility of backward time travel	75

Quick reference — 79

The Garden of Life

The gardener protected his tree,
    called it the Tree of Life.

I had to pay a lot to get its fruit,
    but it didn't satisfy my hunger.

I paid for more of it.
Getting ill of malnutrition
    and staying hungry,

I decided not to eat them anymore.

The gardener became angry and
    together with all eaters
      —suffering from malnutrition and sleep deprivation—
shouted at me:
    once eat the fruit
    always eat the fruit.

How such a garden could possibly be a house of contentment?
Should I escape from this cult?
Or should I examine the tree,
   whether it ever can bring any nutritious fruit?
But how would I know
   whether I'm already poisoned by the gardener,
   and I'm not even aware of it?
Then, what could I do?
...
What would 'I' be?
It is time to figure it out.

Preface

A few years ago, I was eating out at a restaurant when I overheard a man at the table next to me. He shockingly asked the waiter, 'Don't you serve it with rice, bread, potato, or something? How am I supposed to eat it? Am I an animal?' I took a glance at his table; he had ordered a meat dish, which was served without any carbs. Now, he was upset to the point of questioning his existence. I thought to myself, 'What else would you be? Of course, you are an animal. We all are!' But, if I'm questioned, how would I describe what I am?

To find an answer, I embarked on a self-exploratory journey on the meaning of 'I' (and 'time', as it became unavoidable), and this book is a record of it. I enjoyed writing it, and I hope you enjoy reading it.

As a scientist, my usual method of study is by *research* in which *literature review* is a crucial step. In this exploration, however, I have not conducted scientific research. Instead, I have focused on theorizing and sketching hypothetical models without any experimental verification. You may encounter assertive statements; these reflect my thoughts at the time of writing and are subject to change when confronted with convincing arguments.

Moreover, while there may be similarities between the terms I use to propose my ideas and established jargon, my limited familiarity with many of these terms and their precise definitions (if they exist) has led me to prioritize simplicity in language throughout this exploration.

May 2024
Groningen

Outline of the book

This book, in essence, provides two sets of ideas: a brain model and its ability to describe animals' (including humans') perceptions of various experienced phenomena.

Chapter ON I begins by assuming the existence of 'I', which is then dissected into two constituent components: 'my mind' and 'my body'. Given that the construction of 'I' must be rooted in only one of these components, two separate paths are explored. When considering the primacy of the mind, unexpected observations arise, accompanied by an irrefutable explanation: *It is what it is*. Most importantly, this exploration uncovers an inconsistency in the memory available to the mind, rejecting the notion of the mind's primacy.

Following the second path, which considers the primacy of the body, the capacity of an animal to become self-aware is explored. To explain this, a model is proposed that describes the brain as having three layers of memory: the first layer develops muscle memory, the second creates imagined experiences, and the third generates pseudo-experiences. I argue that this model can explain the construction of 'I'.

When exploring the concept of 'I', a fundamental question arises: "What existed before the world began?" To address this, chapter ON TIME delves into the notion of time by defining and examining a hypothetical world. I argue that the concept of time can only exist in the presence of continuously observable changes and that perceived time is dependent on the observer.

Each of these main chapters is supplemented by an appendix that offers further discussions on various topics, such as "Why is language an essential tool for constructing self-awareness?" and "Can we travel backward in time?"

The appendices also delve into intriguing topics, particularly how the proposed brain model can explain a wide range of phenomena we experience—from beliefs and societal behaviors to our perception of time[1] and our capacity to conceive of eternity.

---

[1] For instance, you may have heard that time seems to pass faster as we age because a specific time span (such as one year) constitutes a large portion of a baby's life but only a small portion of an older person's. However, this is merely an observation, not an explanation. In this book, I aim to provide explanations using the brain model developed and presented in chapter ON I.

On I

What am I? What is that entity that I refer to as 'I'? I use it frequently, suggesting I understand what 'I' refers to, but the fact is that its reference is unclear. To find such a reference, I decided to contemplate what 'I' is by searching through my current understanding of this notion without researching and diving into the rich branch of philosophy of mind. In this chapter, I attempt to find an answer to this question.

As a first step to finding out what 'I' refers to, I would like to see in which situations I use it. One is when I engage in conversation with someone. There are also other ways I employ the reference for 'I' in communication. For instance, by raising my hand or pointing towards myself with my index finger, allowing a person standing far away to identify me. Even in stillness, without any external interaction, I can utilize 'I' within my thoughts. This time, the communication is not between two individuals but rather a dialogue within myself. Simply put, I do not require anyone else's presence but myself to use 'I'.

These are some examples of the usage of 'I'. But what does this 'I' refer to? Does it exist only when I engage in communicative interactions? For instance, when I take a walk and have no internal monologue, does 'I' vanish because it is momentarily not in use? No, it would not because even in such moments, if someone asks what I am doing, I will say, 'I am taking a walk.' This implies that the entity I refer to as 'I' is still present, even if I do not explicitly refer to or point to it. This suggests that a communicative interaction is not necessary for its existence. To identify this not-necessarily-communicative-entity, I would scrutinize it through the functions it serves. In the case of communication, the minimum identifier would be the speaker of my inner monologues—my mind. And in the non-communicative case, the minimum identifier is the existence of my body.

What follows is that these two parts—my mind and my body—combine to construct 'I'. One part enables me to observe and interact with the external world, while the other part sporadically emerges and lacks the ability to interact directly with the tangible world. For example, my mind may temporarily vanish while my body remains engaged during countless activities like cooking, watching movies, sleeping, reading books, cycling, and so on. Conversely, I have never engaged in any mental activity that resulted in the disappearance of my body. Even during moments of intense mental focus, my awareness of my body may diminish, yet it remains evidently present, carrying out its functions. These observations suggest a potential hierarchy where one of these parts appears to be superior to the other. But which one would rank higher?

On I

THE ORIGINALITY OF THE MIND

In my teens, I penned a short story featuring a miracle in which the protagonist lost his body, continuing his existence solely through a disembodied mind. It proved to be a harrowing experience for the character. In a pivotal scene, he underwent a resurrection, finding himself inhabiting the body of a person of the opposite sex.

Years later, I realized some similarities between the hierarchy I believed in, as depicted in my story, and the first principle of René Descartes's philosophy, which could be translated into English as *'I am thinking, therefore I exist.'* That is, the true essence of 'I' lies within the realm of the mind, suggesting that the body and the observable world are merely illusory constructs. However, revisiting this notion after two decades, I recognize its inherent problematic nature.

Suppose my body and everything perceivable in the world —hereafter, I refer to it as the *physical* world— are merely illusions created by my mind. Consequently, my body, the other component of 'I', would also be an illusion. In simpler terms, there exists only one true 'I', which is my mind, and the entirety of the physical world, including my body, which is nothing more than a product of my mind's imaginative faculties.[1]

This assumption entails a significant outcome: my mind, as the creator, possesses exceptional knowledge. It has crafted an intricately detailed and coherent world patiently awaiting exploration.

---

[1] Dear reader, you may not appreciate the notion that you are a creation of my mind, but that is an inherent feature of assuming the originality of the mind. Honestly, I share your perspective on this matter, as my own body—a fundamental component of my own 'I'—is imaginary, too!

But what is there to be discovered? The creation or the creator? And by whom? The mind itself or its creations?

This constructed physical world encompasses celestial and interstellar masses gracefully orbiting one another, allowing for the formulation of their precise paths. Also, my mind has fabricated the fields of Physics, Chemistry, and Mathematics, offering me the freedom to delve into whichever subject I desire. My mind employs imaginary figurines and their texts in various languages to share its vast knowledge, enabling me to grasp them to a certain extent. It even playfully puts me on, allowing me to believe that I can choose or invent things, all the while knowing that my mind has already conceived them.

Yet, I failed the course Differential Equations at the university! This failure appears as a perplexing contradiction. On the one hand, my mind has constructed an intricate imaginary world in which I—my body—serve as the sole intermediary to explore its vastness. On the other hand, I am not immune to flaws. I frequently forget things and encounter unknown phenomena, necessitating the need for further study and understanding.

Since the assumption here is that the source of the physical world is 'my mind', it is impossible to consider that there could be any faults within my mind or even its creations. After all, flaws in creations indicate flaws nested in the creator. Instead, this incongruous observation suggests that 'my mind' does not memorize data in the same place that 'my body' has access to. In essence, my mind has crafted an imaginary world in which a portion of it, my body, remains unaware of the other aspects within this physical realm, including the details of my own body.

Before going any further, I should address another question: when has my mind created this world? Was it an instant before the current one? As I write these lines and glance at the written words a minute later, how can I be sure I composed them only a minute ago? Is it not conceivable that my creative mind could conjure up all the intricate details of the physical world, along with all the memories I recall, in an instant?

While such a possibility exists, it is neither verifiable nor provable. In other words, this scenario elicits a *'so what?'* reaction, which renders it unworthy of further investigation. I would set it aside, as it leads nowhere. Instead, I continue my exploration, assuming the existence of time.[2] Yet, there is no possible way to find when my mind has created this physical world, or whether it is continuously manipulating its creatures. There are some philosophical attempts to address this problem, but they all introduce unverifiable planes of existence, which only complicate the understanding of reality and serve as unnecessary additions, extending beyond the limits of the only relatable entity, 'I'. Assuming the originality of mind, whatever cannot coexist within the realm of such a creative mind would swiftly be relegated to the realm of fiction and be rendered unworthy of consideration.

This issue of the origin is the beginning of a list of questions that no answer satisfies them. For example, why does not my mind write these lines by itself, either by moving the pen on paper or by opening a word processor and typing? My mind suggests that it has established specific rules within this physical world and has granted unique attributes to each of its creations. As a result, it consciously refrains from violating its own set of rules.

---

[2] Due to its importance, I reflected on the concept of time in a separate chapter; see page 53.

Curiosity piques within me, and I inquire, 'Why not?'[3] My mind responds, 'Because it desires to navigate and explore the world while abiding by the currently established laws and limitations.' I press on, asking, 'Why?' My mind retorts, 'Why not? *It is what it is.*' And that is an undebatable response.

Another intriguing aspect I have observed is my mind's ability to surprise itself through its own creations. Consider a scenario where an imaginary bee suddenly materializes out of thin air and stings my cheek. Not only does this imaginary bee probably die and its sting causes a physical reaction in my body, it also manages to astonish my mind—the very creator of the bee. This unexpected event prompts me to question, 'Where did this bee come from?' But how is it possible that my mind, the creator of this imaginary world, be caught off guard by its own creation?

One possible explanation is that my mind operates as an observer and driver, overseeing and directing my body's interactions with the physical world. While my mind has the power to generate and shape the world, its experiences are confined to the perspective of my physical body. Therefore, it may seem perplexing that my mind would create illusions that cause harm or discomfort to itself. But why would it engage in self-harming illusions? Regrettably, my mind remains currently unable to provide any satisfying answer except 'it is what it is.'

---

[3] Who is asking this question? Is it my mind itself, posing a question in disguise as if the questioner and the questionee are two separate entities? The only plausible response, assuming the supremacy of the mind, is that the questioning inner voice must be from my mind. So, this questioning process might be part of the intended exploration and discovery, and in essence, it is under the supervision of my mind.

My other related question is why my mind has limited its exploration of the world it has created to only my body. Why does it not venture through the perspectives of other imaginary creatures, be they living or non-living? Why does it not allow itself to experience the world as a bird soaring high in the sky or as a fish gliding through the depths of the oceans? What about the viewpoint of a lost comet, an electron of an atom just passing the event horizon of a black hole, a water molecule experiencing sublimation on a remote planet, or my neighbor?

I have not seen but heard of those who can move things out of their bodies. Yet, even that makes no difference. If people move objects in front of me without moving a single muscle, claiming they do it purely with the power of their mind, that does not affect the power of my mind in the slightest, simply because their entire existence (body and mind) are merely illusions of my mind, which has limited its interactions with the physical world solely through my body. But why?

One possible response is that my mind does indeed engage in such broad explorations, but not within the limitations of the present world. Instead, it conjures up numerous (perhaps infinitely many) alternate physical realms, each offering a distinct perspective to be explored, which may encompass different laws and give rise to diverse types of creatures.

As I contemplate this response, I realize that I must embrace it. At the very least, I am relieved that my mind does not boast about experiencing its created world from a multitude of perspectives at this very moment. Such a claim would suggest that my mind is connected to various bodies at once, yet I cannot recall those bodies as my own. It would imply that my mind maintains constant contact with all its creatures, whether experienced through my body or not. This notion raises a troubling thought, as it would mean that my body is not even the true abode of my mind. If such a claim were made, it would follow that this world was brought into existence by my mind even before it constructed the illusion of my own existence (that is 'I'), and it could continue to exist independently of my presence. Such a claim would dissolve my mind to a mere creative force, a mind detached from my own being, a *mastermind*. And that mind, no longer associated with me, would be the ultimate creator of the world, akin to a deity. The existence of such a realm appears to be necessary. But, this blending seems somehow unavoidable. Let me review some points: earlier, I found that the memories my body has access to do not match the ones my mind claims to create and keep, suggesting that a separate vast memory must exist exclusively for my mind. Yet, my mind limits itself to experience its own created world through my body. Therefore, the mind in the first sentence (with a vast memory) cannot be the same mind in the second sentence (with a limited memory).[4] As a remedy, one could suggest that the first one is the 'mastermind' and the second one is 'my mind'. Simply put, the idea of the originality of the mind does not hold on to itself and leads to introducing a new realm that is marked extraneous and automatically invalidated as it exists out of 'my body' and 'my mind', the only components of the only accepted entity.

And, my questions are not over yet. If all that I perceive is an illusion, what purpose does the experience of this illusory

---

[4] Mistakenly conflating these two minds leads to the notion that *my mind* retains a record of *everything*—at least, anything experienced via 'my body'. This mistake leads to the idea that all these memories persist irrespective of my ability to recall them, and if I forget something, it simply signifies that the corresponding memory is only momentarily inaccessible.

world serve? It is a question that delves into the very essence of my existence, challenging me to contemplate the workings of my mind. After all, it seems unlikely that such a complex and intricately designed world would exist with no purpose.

Perhaps I can attempt to unravel these and the forthcoming questions by identifying all my mind's self-imposed limitations and rules. However, I acknowledge the probability that there may be no ultimate resolution to all the mysteries of my almighty mind besides 'it is what it is.' My mind is a vast and complex entity, filled with wonders and uncertainties. Operating by its own set of rules, many of which remain undiscovered even to itself, my mind possesses the remarkable ability to create, perceive, and astonish itself. Within the realm originating from my mind, questions arise, but definitive answers may remain elusive.

But can I think differently?

The originality of the body

'Follow your heart!' is the first sentence that comes to my mind when thinking about the originality of the body. Not because it holds any special significance, but simply because this command includes a part of my body—my heart. Following this command, should I follow those things that cause my heart to beat faster? Certain things do that as I approach or envision them, and these stimuli evolve over time. It could be a piece of chocolate at one point, a favorite amusement park for a while, perhaps an animation or a book at another time, the person one sees as the life partner, and so on. Now, if it is a piece of cake that quickens my heartbeat, following my heart all the time would make me end up becoming obese or diabetic. Other factors that can usually intensify people's heart rates are any kind of activities (even watching videos) that involve a person in any form of violence; these are something that many strive to avoid.

In essence, I prefer not to follow my heart most of the time. Instead, I aim to act based on reasoning, with the awareness that following my heart is just one element among others.

But where does reasoning take place? Is it not within the mind itself? If so, does it imply that my mind has constructed this physical world, and my imaginary body experiences the illusion of thinking, which indeed happens within my mind? Am I trapped in a loop, affirming the originality of the mind? It should not be so. Let me attempt to carve an escape tunnel.

What if I study the experiences of individuals who have undergone hallucinations or personality changes due to mental or physical conditions? Psychedelic drugs, for example, induce various illusions. Ingesting them might lead to experiences where I

On I

see or hear things that others do not, or feel a connection between all world components, extending beyond the limitations of my body. However, those around me who abstain from such drugs would not share these same experiences. Or, consider the case of Phineas Gage, who survived a severe head injury but underwent a significant personality change. Gage, originally a friendly and responsible railroad construction foreman, had a large iron rod accidentally driven entirely through his head. Despite living for another twelve years post-injury, he was 'no longer Gage'. The accident had a profound impact, transforming him into an angry and impulsive person.

The awareness of such occurrences concerning individuals struggling with diverse conditions was undoubtedly familiar to numerous philosophers throughout history. Yet, the originality of the mind has not been dismissed, as all could be rendered as one's mind's originated fabrications.

What about the revelations of modern biology and neuroscience, which debunked many ancient convictions regarding the functions of the body? We no longer adhere to the belief that the heart is responsible for thinking, nor do we assert that the brain exists to cool down the blood. The notion that the shape of a person's skull reveals clues about their personality has been discredited, and we no longer maintain that men and women possess different brains.[5] These changes are credited to the findings of modern biology and neuroscience, gleaned from the study of the activities of different

---

[5] One might demonstrate that distinct brain regions are activated in similar situations depending on whether the individual is a man or a woman. However, this observation cannot be straightforwardly interpreted as inherent differences between male and female brains. Instead, one may consider that these differences arise due to nurture, including cultural influences.

body parts in diverse situations.

I am now aware that my brain is responsible for intelligence and thought, and damaging it can alter my perception of the world or my personality. Various sensors throughout my body collect diverse data and transmit it to my brain for processing. However, there are numerous ways to trick the brain, aside from directly affecting the brain cells using chemical or physical stimuli, such as psychedelics or hitting with heavy objects. For instance, I can prevent my brain from receiving sensory data using local anesthesia that blocks nerve signals in a specific region. In this scenario, my brain neither receives the sensory information nor interprets it as pain or discomfort, even if received. Moreover, I can confuse my brain in processing the data gathered through my sensory system via sensory illusions, targeting any of the sensors. Examples include Müller-Lyer and Ponzo optical illusions, McGurk and Shepard auditory illusions, and the thermal grill tactile illusion.[6]

All this evidence indicates that I perceive the physical world through my brain. Armed with this knowledge, I can keep my brain happy regardless of the condition of the rest of my body. It only requires convincing my brain that I am eating a piece of cake! This can be achieved by stimulating the parts of my brain responsible for such a sensation. In general, similar methods can be employed to evoke other feelings.

Does this imply that I can only refer to my brain when I want to refer to 'I'? If there is no reasoning within the parts of the body other than the brain, does it mean that life lacks meaning for those body parts? Suppose my entire existence is a compilation of experiences from different components of my body, all processed

---

[6] See chapter Quick reference (page 79) for brief descriptions of these illusions.

within my brain. Then, how can 'I' be constructed within my body? I see this last question as the core challenge, which, if answered, can ultimately suggest a rigorous alternative to the idea of the originality of the mind.

From unicellular to animal

To address this question, certain insights from modern biology become essential. While there is no globally accepted definition, I draw from the cell theory that *the simplest form of life is a single living cell* enveloped by a membrane, creating a boundary between its interior and the external environment. This unicellular organism, residing in a specific habitat, acquires something from its surroundings as the energy source, processes it, and utilizes it to survive and reproduce through cell division.

The primary sources of energy for these cells are either photons, most likely from sunlight, or chemicals, which can be either inorganic (such as hydrogen sulfide or ammonia) or organic (such as sugars or proteins). The latter compounds originate from the remnants of living organisms or products synthesized by them. Cells, in their quest for energy, strive to obtain necessary sources and simultaneously safeguard themselves from becoming the energy source for other organisms—that is, food.

In cases where the energy source is chemical, the cell ingests it by engulfing the chemical within its membrane. Upon sensing the energy source, which can be another living cell, the cell moves its membrane to surround the food. Once the chemical is placed within the membrane and identified as edible, the cell proceeds to digest it.

One mechanism that cells employ to protect themselves from becoming prey is to live together in proximity and form a colonial organism. In a colony of unicells, they establish an enlarged boundary. This connection diminishes the vulnerability of a cell to predation, as the predator may not easily reach the surroundings of a single cell residing within a colony.

Beyond the defense mechanism, such colonies offer additional advantages. The exploration area for finding food expands, and the chance of finding food for the entire colony enhances. Furthermore, there exist various mechanisms for sharing food, with diffusion being the main one.

Living as a colony increases the chance of longevity and obtaining larger meals. However, the entire organism could enhance both factors if it comprises various cells specialized in different tasks. Consider a simple organism with some cells dedicated to collecting and digesting food, while others propel the organism's body toward the food source. To efficiently distribute the digested food throughout the organism, some new specialized cells may be needed to construct a tubelike structure. This new structure facilitates the rapid transport of food to any point throughout the organism's body, overcoming the diffusion limits single-cell organisms face. Consequently, such a multicellular organism would grow as large as it could.

Multicellular organisms have independently evolved many times, giving rise to diverse life forms, including animals on which I will focus in the rest of this text.[7]

---

[7] There are many hypotheses on the origin of multicellular organisms, which do not contribute to this thought exercise, so I will not touch them. Still, that is an exceptionally important topic to explore, as it may show whether all animals have evolved from the same ancestor.

On I

All is by chance

Before going any further, I should acknowledge that everything connected to the originality of the body is a matter of pure chance and random survival. By that, I refrain from using the term 'natural selection' since selection requires intention, which is irrelevant to the impersonal environment (nature) and processes (evolution).

The brain: a model

With the increasing number of specialized cells, a subset of cells became dedicated to regulating and controlling the majority of cells in a body. I refer to these cells as the brain. While for a biologist it might be interesting to study the birth of the brain in animals, my curiosity leads me to explore its potential effects.

I would begin by examining a unicellular organism that navigates toward a source of energy, primarily—and perhaps exclusively—guided by the concentration of the energy source in the food's surroundings. In other words, the organism moves or experiences a drag by gradients of chemicals or temperature in the environment. Now, consider an animal—a larger, multicellular organism—seeking food. Picture a scenario where a small section of the animal's body is exposed to such a gradient, while a significant portion of its body moves in a different direction within a neutral environment. In this situation, the organism would move away from that energy source since most of its mass remains oblivious to the presence of the food. For such an animal, a regulating unit that somehow taps into the experiences of the cells throughout the body becomes vital. This unit, which orchestrates the movement of the entire body toward the food, can aptly be referred to as the brain.[8]

Once the animal reaches the food and eats it, the brain may instruct the animal to take some rest to digest the food and then again instruct it to wander around to find another energy source. Moreover, the brain can give instructions to protect cells against whatever may cause harm, such as too much light or high temperature.

The next evolutionary step for animals involves gathering information through specialized cells that function as sensors sensitive to temperature, vibration, light, certain chemicals, and more. These sensors serve to collect relevant information about food or potential threats from a distance and to transmit it to the brain. For instance, light-sensitive sensors, or eyes, enable the animal to discern food from a considerable distance, granting advantages compared to an animal lacking such sensors. The collaboration between these sensors and the brain is vital for the animal's survival.

The specialized cells play crucial roles in animals' lives, but none in the brain models I will sketch in this work. In the most general sense, I assume three sets of units to build the brain model: a brain (with different subunits that I will describe later), a sensory system (to communicate between different units and subunits), and the rest of the body, which, by interactions with the outer world or within itself, can trigger the sensory system to send signals to the brain and can receive brain's instructions via the sensory system.

---

[8]Of course, there must be some types of cells that can translate certain experiences of each cell and transfer them to the brain cells, and the nervous system is part of this connection. However, as details of these cells do not play a role here, I will leave them out of this work, and only assume their existence.

Figure 1 | Brain Level 1: the simplest brain model for an animal. P|N stands for the processing and the instructing subunits,[9] which together build the brain. The arrow indicates the sensory system, connecting the brain with the rest of the body B. The double-headed arrow is a replacement of two single-headed ones: in the interaction between B and PN units, P receives signals from B, and accordingly, N provides instructions to B.

In the simplest case, as sketched in **Figure 1**, the brain, comprising two subunits—processing P and instructing N—, analyzes the signals and issues instructions, which are then dispatched to the relevant organs via the sensory system.

At this stage, the given instructions are probably a matter of pure chance, and only those lucky animals receiving instructions that keep them alive will survive; they may pass their luck on to their offspring through inheritance. The rest will perish.

The emergence of memory

Brain cells—whatever they are and wherever they are placed—share some characteristics with other cells as a group, not individually. Similar to how a muscle may grow to some extent through regular workouts to better serve the animal, the same principle applies to brain cells. As they continuously receive information from sensory cells, process it, and provide informed instructions, they improve their ability to analyze received information and issue instructions.

---

[9] Hereafter, I refer to these coupled subunits as PN, instead of P|N.

Much like a muscle undergoes change with consistent workouts, brain cells undergo changes through the execution of their tasks.

One notable outcome of such change is what we commonly refer to as memory. When brain cells are consistently exposed to sensory information, the alterations made to both the brain cells and the connections of sensory cells can be so profound that they require no noticeable time to provide relevant instructions. If such an evolution occurs for an animal, it can develop memory, something I assume for the rest of this text.

The primary memory unit (M1), as illustrated in **Figure 2**, suffices for activating new functions, namely, dreaming and reasoning. Yet, a third function is the key to enhancing memory levels, and that is imagination.

DREAMING: Any cell of the body may send false signals to the memory unit, which are then perceived as true, leading to instructions given to the pertinent body cells. This phenomenon is what I call dreaming. In simpler terms, dreaming results from the unintentional stimulation of the memory unit(s) by internally generated signals from any cell of the body, composed of the brain subunits, sensory system, and the rest of the body.

Dreaming predominantly occurs during periods of bodily rest when sensory stimulation is minimal. In such scenarios, slight changes within the cells attached to and within the sensory system—typical behavior for any living cell—might activate the memory unit, resulting in dreaming. One might wonder why this does not happen continuously. The explanation lies in the fact that when the animal is awake and active, externally stimulated signals from the sensory system are way stronger than the internally

Figure 2 | Brain Level 2: the brain model for an animal with the first memory level M1. (left) illustrates M1 during the training process of a task, and (right) displays the trained M1, labeled as $M1_N$. The blue dashed arrow (labeled f) signifies the 'feedback' received. The brain is composed of two units: M1 and PN,[10] the arrows represent the communication passages between the brain and the rest of the body B. In this model, M1 has been trained for a particular set of events, so if triggered by those, it does not interact with PN.

provoked ones. Thus, the relatively weak false signals can only trigger the brain subunits when there are no externally stimulated signals. This is why most animals that experience sleeping dream then.

Moreover, this implies that dreaming is not confined to visual experiences; false signals from any form of the sensory systems (or their relevant memory cells) can activate the memory unit. For instance, it could be an auditory false experience, where the animal hears sounds without any external sources.

Furthermore, to prevent harm, the animal should not act upon the instructions of the brain based on dreams, especially during sleep. While one might argue that nature or evolution designed this mechanism for specific cells to override the brain's instructions

---

[10] It is crucial to understand that M1 is merely a part of the brain trained by repetition of specific tasks. I acknowledge that the figures of this chapter may be misleading by separating subunits of the brain and breaking their hierarchy; but, that is my best try to keep figures concise and straightforward.

during sleep, my perspective leans toward it being a matter of chance: only those sleep-dreaming animals that could remain still have survived.

REASONING: Here, I confine reasoning to induction, and I refer to it as a decision-making tool grounded in gathered evidence: if an animal undergoes a certain experience many times, it induces that the same experience likely occurs the next time.

Consider a hypothetical scenario involving two animals: animal A, the predator, whose prey is animal type B.[11] A relies on its sensory system, for example, its eyes, to locate the position of B. If B moves behind a rock, it becomes hidden from A's view, making it untraceable for A. Now, A, unaware of B's whereabouts, moves in random directions. By chance, A passes by the rock, discovers an animal of type B, and eats it. Assume this scenario repeats several times until A's brain cells shape a memory out of it. Until now, once B hid behind the rock, A cluelessly wandered around. However, from now on, with the formed memory, A first looks behind the rock anticipating finding an animal type B. In essence, A inductively identifies the position of B.[12]

IMAGINATION is the capacity of the brain cells to construct a virtual replica of their surroundings by utilizing information stored as memories. The brain cells retain secondary information derived from firsthand memories and provided instructions. These

---

[11] The next paragraph (imagination) clarifies why here I write 'animal type B' instead of 'animal B'.

[12] That brings the idea that the brain cells give instructions based on two essentially different sources: one is an innate survival kit, and the other is an experimentally adaptive one. However, whether the adaptive kit (memory) can be transferred and implemented within the innate one (instinct) is beyond the scope of this text.

secondary memories, stored by M2 cells, can be enhanced through induction.[13] M2 likely evolves from within $M1_N$ to form secondary memories. When M2 becomes trained and functional, transitioning from M2 to $M2_N$, this memory unit does not necessarily maintain a direct connection with the sensory system but with the PN unit. This unfolds a new capability in the brain, enabling the development of new skills, including the internal triggering of the PN unit.

The internal triggering of the P subunit is what I refer to as imagination,[14] which unfolds as follows: when an externally stimulated sensory system triggers the M1 unit for something it has not been trained for, it dispatches signals to the M2 unit, which may contain pertinent memories from past events. If so, M2 can virtually recreate the external environment, devise various scenarios, prompt PN to analyze them, generate new instructions for each scenario, regulate potential outcomes (informed by the accumulated memory of previous instructions and feedback), and transmit the approved instructions, if any, to M1. After the body executes the instructions, it relays feedback to M1, which in turn communicates feedback to M2. It is worth noting that the feedback signals received by M1 and M2 are not necessarily

---

[13] I cannot think of imagination—at least, in its earliest stage, for example, in babies—prior to the ignition of induction.

[14] One may ask how PN would recognize whether it is triggered by internally or externally stimulated signals. Well, as far as I can understand, it is impossible for it to distinguish the two; that is why our dreams and imaginations can interefer with the autonomic regulation. For example, one may feel an increased heart rate thinking about an infuriating situation. PN may differentiate these two types of signals if it has a signal filtering with an activation threshold since the internally stimulated signals are (probably) weaker than the externally activated ones. While it is not an easy task for PN to make such a distinction, the trained memory cells, however, may be able to make such a distinction.

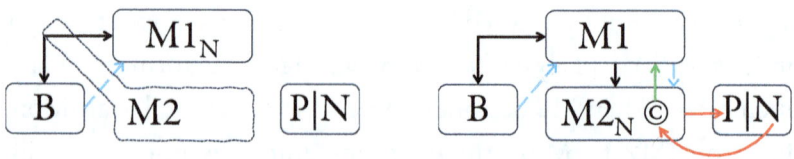

Figure 3 | Brain Level 3: the brain model for an animal with its M2 (left) during and (right) after training. As before, the arrows represent the communication paths between different units of the brain and the rest of the body. Once M2 transforms into M2$_N$, it can communicate with PN by triggering P and receiving instructions from N, which are then to be analyzed and filtered through a *control unit*, depicted by ©. Approved instructions then, if any, will be transmitted to the M1; in such a case, B provides feedback to M1, and M1 then submits the feedback (most probably an altered version of it) to M2$_N$.

identical. **Figure 3** illustrates the placement of the M2 unit before and after training.

To illustrate the imagination process, let us revisit the scenario of A chasing B. In the initial setup, when B took cover behind a rock, A ceased its pursuit because B was no longer within A's line of sight. Despite A having learned that passing the rock would lead to encountering an animal of type B, A could not establish a connection between the two situations.

Now, with a trained M2 unit, A can build an imaginary link between B before and after it goes behind the rock. The key distinction of this new situation is that when B moves behind the rock, A does not merely cross the rock to find an animal of type B but continues chasing the same animal B, even though it is now out of A's sight.

This example might not fully showcase the impact of M2, as A seems to be doing the same thing with or without it. So, allow me to explore another scenario where A still pursues B, but this time, B hides behind a leaf. This is a novel experience for A, lacking any firsthand memories. Without a trained M2, the situation would mimic the previous one: A would aimlessly wander and may or may not discover an animal of type B behind the leaf. However, the trained M2 can leverage its memory of losing and finding B behind the rock. This time, $M2_N$ can form an imaginary replica of B behind the leaf, considering previous movements, speed, and other features. Communicating this imaginary replication to the P subunit, the N subunit guides A to move behind the leaf purposefully, searching for B. If A locates B, it reinforces $M2_N$ for such imaginative processes in subsequent explorations.

Crucially, $M2_N$ develops a control unit (depicted by © in **Figure 3**) powered by the accumulated memories, primarily aiming to prolong the animal's life span. This implies that if $M2_N$ envisions a scenario in which the given instructions might harm the animal, the control unit filters that instruction out and transmits only ones beneficial for a specific task.

Continuing with this line of thought: after a sequence of A's successes attributed to the information provided by $M2_N$, a tertiary layer of memory (the M3 unit) can develop, containing data from all these experiences, which maintains connections with both M2 and PN units. Subsequently, M3 can interact with M2 and PN and oversee instructions at a higher level than the control unit of M2. **Figure 4** illustrates the placement of M3 in the memory layer.

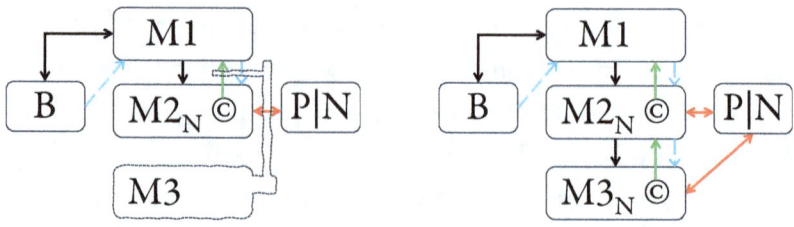

Figure 4 | Brain Level 4: the brain model for an animal with 3 levels of memory (left) during and (right) after the training of its M3. The interactions of M2 and M3 with PN should be read as shown in **Figure 3**, that is, the memory unit(s) receive instructions of N by their control unit for further processing; here, I merely used double-headed arrows for brevity.

Now with a $M3_N$ unit, we can continue with the scenario of A chasing B. When A encounters a new situation (for instance, when B hides inside a tube), the $M2_N$ unit, lacking memory of such an event, struggles to form an accurate imaginary representation. In this scenario, $M2_N$ might generate an image of B behind the tube instead of inside it, leading A to failure. However, with the intervention of the trained M3, it can prompt $M2_N$ to create new virtual images of B's position. That does not happen because $M3_N$ knows where B is; instead, it refers to the memories in which B could hide but not vanish. So, by experience and chance, $M3_N$ may keep A around the tube. At the same time, $M2_N$ generates new pictures of B's possible positions, which are then processed by P, and N provides A with instructions to move in certain directions.

If A succeeds in finding B, this experience reinforces $M3_N$, solidifying the idea that B should always be close to somewhere it disappears. Additionally, M2 stores a new possibility for where B may hide; this means that M2 transforms to $M2_N$ for that type of scenario. Conversely, if A fails to find B, this setback may weaken

On I

$M3_N$, but perhaps not the M2.[15]

At this point, the complexity of this brain model suffices to give rise to what I am seeking: the 'I'.

Adequacy of the brain model[16]

Table 1 (see page 26) summarizes animals' functionality based on the presented brain model. In the Functionality column, the sign '−' indicates a brainless organism's features and functionalities, and '+' points to the newly added brain units and their pertinent functionalities. The features added by '+' remain for the next brain levels. In contrast, unless explicitly mentioned, those features assigned with '−' would vanish. For example, 'random walks' never disappear, while 'uncoordinated movements' vanishes at the brain level 1.

Reviewing the features of the brain at each level, it can be clarified why introducing a quaternary memory is unnecessary. The M3 unit incorporates the ability to construct imagination within past imaginations; in simpler terms, M3 is self-referenced, and adding any other memory units would not enhance the model's complexity.

The emergence of the self-referenced M3 enables the animal to imagine on demand. In essence, a trained M3 can expand its imagination without relying on new information from M1 or M2. It can also communicate with PN, either with or without the assistance of M2. This means that an animal equipped with M3

---

[15]This behavior resembles what we commonly refer to as self-confidence.
[16]Hereafter, I use Mx interchangeably with Mx_N, for $x = 1, 2$, and 3.

Table 1 | The functionality of animals at different brain levels. See page 25 for the description of the signs '−' and '+' of the Functionality column.

Brain level	Brain unit	Functionality
0	—	− Random walks
		− Moving by chemical and/or temperature gradients
		− Uncoordinated movements
1	P|N	− Random walks
		− Moving by chemical and/or temperature gradients
		+ Birth of the sensory system
2	+M1	− Random walks
		+ Induction
		+ Dreaming
3	+M2	− Random walks
		+ Imagination within past experiences
4	+M3	− Random walks
		+ Imagination within past imaginations

can imagine something distant from its external world, submit it to P for processing, and monitor the instructions provided by N.

The capacity to imagine things without a connection to the physical world, bypassing the sensory system and M1 (and even M2), allows M3 to experience an existence independent of the outer world—an existence we commonly refer to as the mind.

The ability of M3 to generate imaginations within past imaginations allows it to create events for M2 and PN that have no connection to the physical world. Hereafter, I refer to this concept of M3-generated experiences as *pseudo-experiences*. The primary tool for M2 to differentiate between physical-based experiences and pseudo-experiences is its expectations, shaped by past encounters.

Before proceeding, it is essential to note that although the imaginations of M3 can detach from the animal's physical-based experiences, M3 has been trained based on such information. Therefore, while M3 can imagine things not-yet-(pseudo-)experienced, these imaginations may only gradually transition from familiar items to unfamiliar ones. However, since imagination and dreaming can be intertwined (or even happen simultaneously), the progress of pseudo-experiencing of novel things (like various concepts) can speed up by practice as it makes a reinforcing feedback loop within distinct memory units.

The impacts of the nested memory units

In the section 'the emergence of memory' (page 17), I outlined three key functions facilitated by M1: dreaming, reasoning, and imagination. Further exploring the latter, I introduced two nested memory units (M2 and M3) and their contributions to expanding the animal's brain capacity.

Each memory unit offers various abilities to the animal, enhancing reasoning and dreaming processes, too. For instance, M2 enables expectation and spatial visualization.[17] Combining these two, M2 can imagine diverse not-yet-experienced scenarios, communicate with PN, analyze (multiple) instructions, and select one or more actions using its control unit. This form of M2-driven imagination can be termed physical-based thinking, as schematically shown in **Figure 5**. With practice, M2 becomes adept at anticipating such scenarios, allowing it to promptly signal M1 to act based on pre-approved instructions and expected outcomes.

The capabilities enabled by M3 are accociated with abstract concepts, which do not necessarily comply with physical-based experiences. As a result, they can significantly influence the dreaming experience of an animal. This brief note highlights the impacts of M2 and M3 on the processes of reasoning and dreaming.

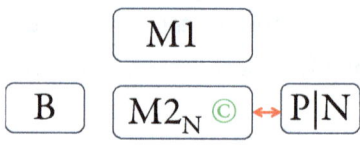

Figure 5 | The brain model for M2-based imaginations.

---

[17] M2 can reproduce mental images, sounds, or any of the five senses, which may or may not be as vivid as received by the signals from the sensory system. You may search for *hyperphantasia* and *aphantasia* for further information on this topic.

The advent of nested memory units extends the scope of reasoning methods from induction (M1) to abduction (M2) and deduction (M3). Previously, I explained how the emergence of M1 enables the use of induction to draw conclusions based on observations. With the addition of M2, which facilitates the construction of phyusical-based imaginations, animals can extend their reasoning to abduction: generating plausible conclusions by combining observations and expectations. If M3 is at work, the expectations of M2 can extend into the non-physical realm of M3.

Subsequently, M3 enables animals to engage in deduction, drawing conclusions from pure pseudo-experience-based imaginations. In essence, the ability of M3 to generate pseudo-experiences and directly interact with PN empowers animals to conduct deductive reasoning. For further details, refer to the section 'the fictitious power of M3' on page 40.

While M1 is primarily associated with basic dreaming, centered on muscle memory, M2 and M3 introduce new dimensions to animal dreaming. M2 enriches dreams by constructing simulations of past experiences, such as visualizing scenes, and broadens them to unfamiliar yet physically plausible scenarios. These dreams, though still fragmented, become more sustained due to M2's ability to anticipate events. This unintentionally creates a virtual world resembling the animal's experiences, allowing its memory units to explore within. For example, a dream might reflect recent experiences, enhancing the animal's learning process.

If an animal equipped with only M1 and M2 could share its dreams, it would accurately convey its perceptions of them. Simply put, interpreting these dreams would be straightforward. For instance, if we observe an animal dreaming of running through a tunnel, we know that the dream is limited to that scenario, perhaps involving searching for a way out. Experiencing such dreams could trigger related memories, potentially evoking physiological responses like increased heart rate. However, we would not interpret the animal's perception of that dream to include abstract concepts like fear or transitions, or physically unrelated experiences such as powerfully embarking on a journey, as those are attributes of M3.

The role of M3 extends beyond dream interpretation, which most probably happens once the animal is awake. As far as I can think of for now, M3 serves two key functions in dreaming: decision-making and dream world fabrication. With M3, decisions in dreams are no longer bound by physical experiences; abstract concepts like bravery and fear can influence choices. Additionally, M3 can influence the content of the dream world generated by M2. Thus, dreams may occur in worlds with elements unrelated to the physical realm, such as encountering mythical creatures like sphinxes or lamassus[18]. Further discussion on dreaming can be found in the section 'sleep terror & lucid dream' on page 45.

Foundations of 'I'

My body: An animal equipped with M3 possesses a mind. But does this animal now refer to itself as 'I'? To recap, 'I' comprises both 'my body' and 'my mind'. At the brain level 1, with the presence of only the PN unit, the animal can identify the parts under its control, that is, its body. While the animal may control its body, at this level, it cannot conceptualize that as 'my body'.

As for now, it seems challenging for me to envision an animal without a trained M3 unit referring to any part of itself as 'my body'. This does not imply that such animals do not value their

---

[18] See chapter Quick reference (page 79) for brief descriptions of these creatures.

bodies; they do. Even with a PN unit, an animal can sense and react without forming the concept of 'my body'. However, M3 can generate an imaginary existence distinct from the animal's body. As the M3 unit develops, it strengthens until it submits signals to M2 almost as potent as those from M1. This marks the moment for M3 to assert its own existence. Functioning as one entity, the cells of the M3 unit construct one imaginary existence of mind.[19] Additionally, as M3 increasingly influences the animal's behavior and (re)actions, it can override M2's commands, virtually send signals to M1 unit, and seize control of the animal's body. Whether acknowledged or not, M3 experiences direct control of the animal's body.

With such a power, M3 considers the animal's body under its control. What else falls under its direct control? Nothing; its controlling power is confined to the animal's body, and this realization is the origin of establishing a boundary for what it claims as '*my* body'.[20]

MY MIND: Up until now, the animal under scrutiny has had limited interactions with other animals; I have only illustrated a scenario of *A* chasing *B*. In such circumstances, I do not foresee the M3-created mind, which asserts the animal's body as 'my body', naming itself 'my mind'. This can only take place in interactions involving more than one animal with developed M3 units.

During these interactions, animals enabled with M3 realize that there are other minds, too, claiming their own bodies. An integral

---

[19] Probably disjointed operations between cells of a trained M3 unit result in claiming separate minds within a body.
[20] That limit, and consequently the understanding of 'my body', would, of course, be expanded by augmenting the body.

aspect of this interaction is that these minds must present their existence to each other; otherwise, there is no conceivable way for a mind to identify other minds. Only when a mind perceives the existence of another mind can it establish the boundaries of its directives, reiterating what it had claimed before: 'my body'. Now, in such interactions, the mind recognizes its own presence, and to assert its position in that interaction, it refers to itself as '*my* mind'. The kind of interaction that prompts a mind to express itself to other minds is *language*,[21] enabling self-recognition and allowing a mind to feel a sense of possession and label itself 'my mind'.

Now, 'my mind' and 'my body', as asserted by a trained M3 unit of an animal, give rise to what I was searching for, the familiar 'I'.

---

[21] For a discussion on why I find language is required for this interaction, refer to the section 'why language?' on page 36.

On I

THE ORIGIN, THE CREATION

In this work, I aimed to delineate a hierarchy between the mind and the body, ultimately reaching a conclusive resolution. The premise driving this exploration hinges on the notion that 'I' is composed of only two components: a physical body and a non-physical mind. Under this foundational assumption, my life experiences are channeled solely through what I identify as 'I', comprised exclusively of 'my mind' and 'my body'. Any proposition suggesting additional realms or existences would thus be extraneous and erroneous.

Assuming the originality of the mind signifies that it must have existed prior to the existence of the physical world. This notion suggests a profoundly self-centered perspective revolving around the concept of 'I'. To justify this stance, numerous inquiries must be addressed, and each answer may ultimately boil down to '*It is what it is,*' which I must passively accept devoid of any motivation to seek deeper understanding. Furthermore, my mind has devised countless incidental exceptions to maintain a sense of surprise, rendering attempts to unravel the mysteries of life futile. This also implies that I possess neither freedom nor will within the confines of my mind-crafted existence.

However, none of these arguments disprove the originality of the mind, as they could all be constructs of my own mind. What undermines this argument is the phenomenon of *forgetfulness*, which contradicts the notion of a boundless and eternally present memory accessible to my mind. This contradiction, wherein memory should be available to a singular entity—my mind—while is not, reveals the flawed nature of this reasoning, thereby challenging the assumption of the originality of the mind.

The alternative perspective is to assume the originality of the body, which implies that the physical world exists independently of my presence, suggesting that my body is the source of my mind.

Embracing the notion that my existence originates from my body resolves many mysteries at once. It grants me free will[22] and the capacity to study and explore any component of the physical world using the necessary means. I am no longer the center of the world, and my body as well as you, my esteemed reader, are not mere illusions of my mind. This perspective equips me with the tools to scientifically investigate the realm of the physical world, offering more straightforward, clearer, and coherent explanations for observed phenomena. For instance, the surprise caused by a bee's sting arises simply from my lack of awareness of its presence. It becomes simpler to explain why my mind is confined within my body. With unknown phenomena, scientific methods can be employed to study them, understand the involved mechanisms, explain and predict them by various theories, and adjust the discussions and conclusions as needed. All this contradicts the perspective of the originality of mind, where answers perpetually await discovery, often with the ever-possible disheartening response of 'it is what it is.'

---

[22] A separate thinking session is required to explore different views toward free will and determinism.

On I—*Further discussions*

This appendix presents topics introduced earlier but were not essential for the arguments. Here, the focus is on three main areas:

- *'Why language?'* discusses the necessity of language in empowering a mind's self-consciousness,

- *'The fictitious power of M3'* presents some features enabled by M3, and

- *'Phenomena'* exemplifies how the presented brain model can elucidate various phenomena.

Throughout this chapter, I use 'BL' to abbreviate 'brain level'.

WHY LANGUAGE?

Discussing the foundations of 'I'—the paragraph 'my mind' on page 31—I claimed that language is the type of interaction required to allow a mind to become self-aware, and one may rightfully ask 'Why language?'. The first step in addressing this question is for me to depict what I mean by language. Let me begin with two features: language involves intentional use and conveys imagination.

With these features, animals at BLs 0, 1, and 2 lack the capacity to comprehend language because they lack imagination. On the other hand, animals at BLs 3 and 4 can imagine things and, therefore, can perceive language.

The main difference in the concept of language between the BL3 and BL4 animals lies in its extent. BL3 animals are confined to their physically activated experiences, whereas BL4 animals have no such limitation.[1] This provides another clue about language: it is an invention, initially experienced by chance and then reinforced through repetition. Let me illustrate this with a simple scenario.

Consider two animals with trained M2 units: A and A^*. The very first time A performs a task (T) that elicits a favorable reaction (R) from A^*, A may not even register that chain of events as it lacks memory of it. Only through repetition may A memorize it with its M1 unit. Let us assume such repetition occurs.

Up to this point, it is possible that A performed T only by chance or for some externally activated and unintentional reasons, no matter what. However, with the repetition of the entire chain through a trained M1 unit, A's M2 can be established by incorporating interactions between M1 and A's body and the received feedback. Once M2 becomes robust enough to directly

---

[1] Whether BL4 animals realize their potential in using language is fundamentally a different story.

On I—Further discussions

send signals to PN, $\mathcal{A}$ is prepared to perform $\mathcal{T}$ to receive $\mathcal{R}$ without external stimuli.[2]

An essential aspect of crafting language is that both $\mathcal{A}$ and $\mathcal{A}^*$ must create a memory of the chain of events. Consequently, $\mathcal{A}$ learns that $\mathcal{T}$ leads to $\mathcal{R}$ from $\mathcal{A}^*$'s response, and $\mathcal{A}^*$ learns that $\mathcal{A}$'s performance of $\mathcal{T}$ results in $\mathcal{R}^*$, the reaction of $\mathcal{A}^*$ to $\mathcal{T}$ as perceived by $\mathcal{A}^*$.[3] Recall that $\mathcal{A}$ initially performed $\mathcal{T}$ in the presence of $\mathcal{A}^*$ by chance. Now, consider what happens if $\mathcal{A}$ performs $\mathcal{T}$ seeking $\mathcal{R}$ by an intentional prompt from its M2. Would it be qualified as a linguistic act? I guess that depends on the school of linguistic theory one tends to, a topic beyond the scope of the current attempt. For reference, let me term it *Primary Language*. Such language cannot be invented but can only be formed by pure chance and through training of M2 units.

One evident characteristic of primary language is that its range of possible $\mathcal{T}$s is limited to commonly shared experiences of $\mathcal{A}$ and $\mathcal{A}^*$. If language is perceived merely as a tool for communicating based on tangible experiences, then primary language qualifies as a language.

Now, consider $\mathcal{B}$ and $\mathcal{B}^*$, two BL4 animals, assuming they have already formed a primary language. Each could have its own unique M3-originated pseudo-experiences, which are not directly shareable with the other due to the lack of external appearance.

Take $\mathcal{B}$ with a specific M3-generated pseudo-experience: finding a good meal beyond its body's reach. $\mathcal{B}$ pseudo-experiences a task

---

[2] No language has emerged yet. At this stage, an animal of type $\mathcal{A}$ can become superstitious; see page 43.
[3] $\mathcal{R}$ and $\mathcal{R}^*$ are objectively a single event, and subjectively two events experienced by $\mathcal{A}$ and $\mathcal{A}^*$, respectively.

T in which itself and B^* collaborate to catch that food. B's mind figures out that B^*'s body is beyond B's control. Moreover, B's pseudo-experience of T is not shared with B^*, so they have not formed any primary language for T. Now, B would start sending some signals to communicate its pseudo-experience with B^*. The signals possibly contain some elements of their primary language and maybe new signs. B^* receives them, but it would be next to impossible for B^* to directly interpret those signals to grasp B's mind's pseudo-experience. Sooner or later, B^* begins to interpret those signals by creating some imagination out of them, makes an interpretation, reacts, and takes the initial steps in devising a *Secondary Language*, a process that takes time for B and B^* to accomplish. Eventually, that will happen—as has happened. An established secondary language performs as an interface for B and B^* to share their pseudo-experiences.

In a scenario where B demands something from B^* and B^* reacts accordingly every single time, B has absolutely no tool to comprehend the existence of B^*'s mind. B might even conclude that B^* is, in fact, part of its own body; only to issue orders, it must use a certain tool, the secondary language, which was akin to training or gaining control over part of its body. Therefore, B might regard B^*'s body as its own possession and label it 'my body'.

I consider this scenario rather rare since B^* has its own pseudo-experiences, too, worth sharing with B. In another extreme, there is this scenario where B^* demands something from B, and B agrees with every single received request and reacts in a way B^* expects. In this case, B may find B^*'s signals peculiar but cannot grasp their origin; instead, B experiences what we commonly refer to as inspiration.

On I—Further discussions

The intriguing scenario arises when *B* asks for something and *B** requests another. The clash between *B*'s and *B**'s minds is the focal point here. That experience is pivotal for *B* and *B** to comprehend a mind beyond their own existence, and this revelation takes place only through dissent. It is when a mind begins to refer to itself as '*my* mind'.[4] I assume that the essentiality of the secondary language in constructing 'my mind' is now clear.

---

[4] That may seem redundant, but it is still not a bad idea to mention that we, humans, do not need to invent a secondary language from the basis anymore. Instead, we learn it from other members of our communities and gradually expand it.

THE FICTITIOUS POWER OF M3

Some characteristics of BL4 animals enhanced by M3 include the ability to directly submit signals to PN, either independently or in collaboration with M2, and the capacity to overrule M2's instructions. To illustrate this concept, consider a physically harmful experience that all units interpret as pain, such as touching a thorn. While the physical-based instructions might prompt screaming and jerking away the endangered body part, M3 can intervene and revoke all instructions by projecting some pseudo-experiences. For instance, M3 might imagine that a talking flower blooms if the thorn cuts a finger and blood droplets fall on the soil. If so, is it not worth exploring? This type of overruling behavior can also shed light on belief-based activities, such as sacrifice. **Figure 6** illustrates a relevant brain model.[5]

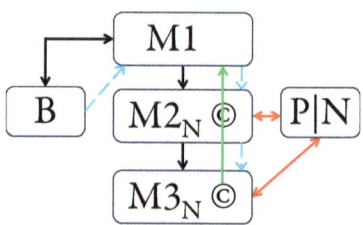

Figure 6 | The brain model where M3 overrules M2's instructions.

Another form of interaction between memory units occurs when M3 triggers M2 without any external stimulator. This activates M2, in collaboration with PN, to examine hypothetical situations created by M3 (that is, pseudo-experiences) and provide

---

[5]The overruling of M2 is also possible. For example, M3 gives instructions based on some ethical principles, but M2 may refuse them due to the possible harm that those instructions may cause.

endorsed decisions, which are then reviewed by M3 to offer feedback to M2. The review would be belief-based, for example, from viewpoints backed with ethical, religious, or scientific arguments and interpretations. Engaging in thought experiments exemplifies this information exchange, as depicted in **Figure 7**, illustrating the workflow for such an interaction between M3, M2, and PN units.

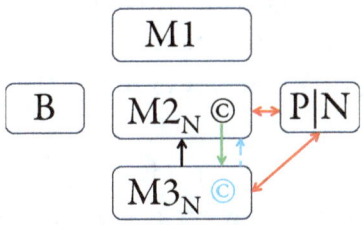

Figure 7 | The brain model for M3-initiated interaction with M2.

A subset of the abovementioned interaction occurs when M3 directly engages with PN cells with limited exchanges with M2, as illustrated in **Figure 8**. This workflow is pertinent to abstract thinking, where M2's involvement is mainly to assist M3 in the imagination process. For instance, if M3 envisions the number 365, M2 may contribute a vision solely to aid M3 in working with that number.

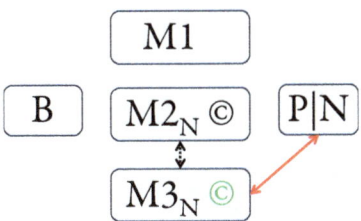

Figure 8 | The brain model for M3-initiated interaction with PN.

Phenomena

Assuming the originality of the mind, most explanations for various phenomena ultimately lead to a dead end of 'it is what it is.' To circumvent this, questions could be directed towards a necessary mastermind, effectively evading the consequences of such an assumption altogether. However, a more robust approach entails rejecting the presumption of the mind's primacy and instead embracing the originality of the body.

In this section, I aim to elucidate several phenomena and observations by means of my brain model, providing only a few examples, namely *supersition, mirror self-recognition test, sleep terror & lucid dream, colonies & societies,* and *brain damage*. Moreover, I can imagine the presented brain model could potentially serve as a foundation for constructing digital animals with a digital brain, but I defer this exploration to future works.

On I—Further discussions

Superstition

Consider a BL3 animal A with a trained M2 in performing a task T by intentionally sending signals to its PN, expecting to receive a reward R. In this scenario, A could establish a belief that performing T under certain conditions would result in a reward R. Even if A does not achieve R, it might experiment with variations of T, leveraging its M2 to construct imaginations. However, A's explorations would not go too far, as M2's imagination is bound by physical experiences.

But what if the animal is equipped with an M3 unit? In that case, if the animal performs T and does not receive R, it could still form a belief that there is surely a variation of T to obtain R, as theoretically, there is no border to limit the imaginations of a BL4 animal.[6]

One form of such baseless belief is what we commonly refer to as superstition, and all of this unfolds before the advent of language.

---

[6] A BL4 animal can even imagine physically impossible variations of R for achieving which it must perform physically impossible variations of T.

Mirror self-recognition test

Consider a BL3 animal A that encounters its reflection in a mirror (A^*). In such a case, A can recognize that it has control over the movements of A^* without necessarily grasping the concept of a mirror and reflection. A experiences only a coordination between A and A^* movements. Through its M2, A might even identify specific features in A^*'s body. We might observe such identifications through A's reactions in interactions with A^* and label it as self-recognition. However, in A's M2 unit, A^* might be considered merely as part of A's body, but not its image reflected on a mirror.

On I—Further discussions

Sleep terror & lucid dream

In section 'the emergence of memory' (page 17), I posited that M1 alone could facilitate dreaming, with M2 provides the capacity for imagination, enhancing dreams' vividness and relevance to the physical outer world. Furthermore, the imaginations generated by M2 (processed by PN) enable practicing not-yet-experienced events, preparing the animal for quicker reactions in such scenarios. If an animal is equipped with M3, this unit can elevate dreams to realms unrelated to externally stimulated experiences.

A miscoordination between the memory units can result in sleep terror or lucid dreaming. Consider a state where some parts of M2 and M3 continue sleeping (that is, they are involved in an unintentional and uncontrolled activity) while M1 becomes active in responding to physical stimuli, infusing the received signals of the sensory system into the continued dreaming of M2 and M3. Under such a condition, the animal may face confusion due to a blend of sensory system-activated experiences and memory-generated pseudo-experiences, such as receiving physically activated visual signals intertwined with imaginary figures. This confusion, which not necessarily but can be horrifying, is what we refer to as sleep terror.

In a different state, consider M1 and M3 remains asleep, while M2 identifies some inconsistencies between what it experiences (the dream) and its expectations. Upon this abductively reasoned identification, M2 may become aware of being in a dream, which is the onset of lucid dreaming.

Colonies & societies

On the topic of unicellular organisms, I previously introduced the concept of colonies, where cells attach to each other, forming a collective life. This notion extends to multicellular organisms at any brain level, although with differences from various perspectives. While a single multicellular organism can be compared to a colony where all cells benefit mutually, colonies can also be constructed from multiple multicellular organisms. Building such colonies of animals with BLs of 0 to 2 is like the ones from unicellular, that is, by pure chance. The interesting colonies—interesting for me—are those formed by animals with the BLs 3 and 4. Such colonies may be referred to as societies, but since 'society' has its already established definition(s), I would continue with the term 'colony' to avoid confusion.

Brain level 3: A colony of BL3 animals differs fundamentally from colonies of BL2 animals. In the latter, individual actions are guided by random walks and past experiences. Success in such a colony is essentially a matter of chance. However, BL3 animals can construct a primary language and use it to drive the success of the colony. Although chance remains a significant factor in the formation of a primary language, once established, colony members can sustain it and leverage it to their advantage, establishing new rules and habits for instinct-driven actions, such as teamwork or hierarchy.

This transformative change effectively turns the colony into an organism for itself, comprising multiple multicellular organisms assuming roles and actively communicating to ensure the colony's success.

On I—Further discussions

BRAIN LEVEL 4: A colony formed by BL4 animals reaches a distinct level where its shape is not confined to shared experiences. Each individual can contribute unique elements to the colony, which may be either beneficial or detrimental to the colony as a whole or to specific members. Such a colony possesses a unique feature that cannot be traced in other colonies: *culture*. Looking up the meanings of culture, you will end up with a wide range of definitions. So, I need to define what I mean by this word: here, I refer to culture as a set of acts and beliefs that may have originated for a function (supported by M2) but persisted for their forms (supported by M3), irrespective of practicing the function.

There are more features to such a colony, like love, bravery, self-sacrifice, suicidal operations, and other societal acts.[7] While BL3 animals might display similar behaviors—observable for their signs—they would not take actions unrelated to their direct experiences of the outer world. So, they would not consider concepts such as love, bravery, or death when making a decision since these either have no direct outer world reflections or, in the case of death (for example, in a suicide attack), are beyond any experience. Yet, a BL4 animal may project its own beliefs onto observed acts of animals of other BLs.

In short, BL3 animals act based on their experienced observations. BL4 animals behave differently, as their pseudo-experiences (stories and narratives) play far more important roles in their decision-making processes.

---

[7] I intentionally highlighted features that lack clear definitions or could harm colony members. Regarding death, no living organism can directly undergo and learn from it to use that experience for any coming decisions, as death halts all actions of the dead organism.

Nature and Nurture

It is widely recognized that both nature and nurture contribute to shaping the behavior of individuals in human societies. But how does this dynamic unfold in general terms for animals with different brain levels?

All brain-powered animals begin their journey from BL1, where a PN unit oversees the animal's general activities. The memory units may develop from certain cells within the matured PN unit. Various factors influence the behavior of the pre-memory PN unit, including inherited genes, chemical substances received by the fetus and newborn, and the composition of the intestinal microbiome. The PN unit operates without training, underpinning the animal's innate behavior.

In subsequent stages, the memory units are systematically trained through the direct or indirect interactions of PN with the external world through a feedback loop. The presence of feedback in memory unit training underscores the impact of nurture in shaping the animal's behavior.[8] However, the continued presence of PN highlights the significant influence of nature.

---

[8] The emergence of different memory levels significantly contributes to an animal's training. For instance, attempting to construct a primary language with an animal lacking M2 or training an animal without M3 to behave ethically would be futile.

On I—Further discussions

BRAIN DAMAGE

I have constructed all my arguments based on my brain model, which in its full version comprises a core PN unit and three layers of memories. In this final note, I would like to explore the unsettling notion of brain damage. Let me explain what I mean by that. Consider an animal of any brain level suddenly, permanently, and fully losing one or some of its brain units.[9] What would be the impact of such a change on the animal?

Considering all possibilities would yield too many options, some of which closely resemble each other. I begin with basic scenarios. Generally, when an animal loses only its final brain unit, its brain power downgrades to that of an animal of the previous brain level. For instance, if a BL4 animal loses its M3, its brain functions similar to a BL3 animal, and so forth. Therefore, if a BL1 animal loses its PN, its brain power regresses to that of a BL0 animal, reaching the base state.[10]

A crude failure is the loss of the PN, resulting in the animal's inability to process new information and provide instructions accordingly. Consequently, if an animal loses its PN unit, it may continue living in familiar situations if its memory units function as before. Yet, most probably, the animal's behavior alters drastically since the PN is also responsible for instinctive and innate behaviors. Moreover, the loss of the PN in an animal reliant on functioning of this unit may lead to the animal's death. For these

---

[9] I will not address any partial brain damages, as they are too complicated and impossible to be addressed in any general sense.

[10] This conversion to the base state might sound akin to a vegetative state or brain death; however, I refrain from drawing any connections as these terms have distinct medical meanings and implications, while the base state described here is based solely on my hypothetical brain model.

reasons, I will continue examining other possibilities, assuming a functioning PN unit.

With this assumption, the simplest failure may occur for a BL2 animal losing its M1. It would lose its muscle memory and the ability to dream and to reason inductively. Therefore, if the animal is not in a dangerous environment and does not rely on rapid muscle memory-based actions, it can continue its life.

The next failure corresponds to a BL3 animal losing its M1. This animal can still dream, imagine, and engage in inductive and abductive reasoning. It can plan and has the potential to develop a primary language. What it loses is its ability for rapid muscle memory-based actions and behaviors. Nonetheless, it can still exhibit relatively swift reactions by training its M2 for familiar situations and preparing for not-yet-experienced ones through imagination. This animal may realize the absence of certain behaviors it once took for granted. For example, it may take longer to react to danger or experience less joy from eating a meal if that joy is associated with a distant inactive memory stored in M1.

The final instances of failure concern BL4 animals with intact M3. In the event of memory loss, these animals endure mental anguish as they are unable to align their actions with their self-perception.

These animals may encounter three distinct scenarios of memory loss. The first involves losing M1. This condition mirrors that of a BL3 animal losing its M1. Its ability for rapid muscle memory-based (re)actions ceases, yet it retains the capacity for dreaming, imagining, and reasoning (in all three forms).

The second scenario of failure involves losing both M1 and M2. In this case, the animal loses its muscle memory, its source of physical-based imagination, and all dependent capabilities. Such an animal becomes unable to engage in spatial imaginations or prepare for unfamiliar physical-based situations, that is, considering various possibilities of an event and selecting the most favorable one(s). Most critically, it may lose the ability to interpret incoming signals from its sensory system. Essentially, it loses its ability to categorize and label anything based on physical stimuli. For instance, while its eye may receive signals stimulated by light reflected from an object, the animal may not recognize receiving these signals altogether as it lacks the established pathways.[11] Consequently, the animal's body can continue its life as long as its PN assists and its M3 creates a realm isolated from external interaction. In the extreme scenario, M3 generates the illusion of a disembodied mind, which may perceive itself as impotent or omnipotent.

The last type of memory loss for a BL4 animal involves losing only its M2, resulting in a peculiar condition. While the animal retains its extensive M1-based abilities, the absence of M2 prevents the identification of signals from the sensory system. Consequently, the animal cannot recognize or label the received signals. This scenario is distinctive because the signals still stimulate M1, eliciting responses that may conform to peer expectations, thereby (possibly) masking the absence of M2. However, the animal experiences significant mental distress, as it cannot engage in any physical-based imagination while its M3 is functional and partially connected to its sensory system (and the rest of its body) through its functioning M1. Despite M3's attempts to stimulate the lost M2 in order to create physical-based imaginations, this endeavor proves futile, intensifying the confusion. In the absence of both

---

[11] One might consider that although M3 is not directly linking the sensory system to PN, it could potentially experience and adapt to these signals. However, this notion contradicts the concept of memory loss because such adaptation would essentially transform M3 into M2. However, the scenario I am exploring in the text here pertains to the irreparable loss of M2.

M1 and M2 (as mentioned in the previous paragraphs), M3 eventually creates a disembodied mind out of itself. In the scenario of this paragraph, however, M3 recognizes the existence of the body but with no clear image to exercise its power on. In other words, although abstract concepts and ideas remain accessible to M3, allowing for abstract thinking on various topics, it does not empower M3 to rule over M1 (and other bodily organs), as M3 cannot make sense of unlabeled signals submitted directly by M1.

On Time

I came across the concept of time while contemplating 'I', particularly in discussions centered on the assumption of the originality of the mind, in which context, the non-physical (master)mind is the creator of the world, and some time-related questions such as 'What was there before the inception of the physical world?' or 'When did the (master)mind onset the creation?' may arise. One may imagine that there was not and could not be any physical (or even non-physical) existence except for the mind itself, and the physical world is indeed a manifestation of that mind upon its self-recognition. The other approach is to stop questioning entirely and simply accept the invincible response, 'It is what it is.' After all, a proponent of a (master)mind may ask, 'How is it possible to create the physical world without a mastermind?' But this question is as legitimate as asking, 'How is it possible to create a mastermind without the physical world?' One common aspect of these questions refers to the time before the creation of the realm under inquiry. Therefore, it is essential to clearly identify what we refer to by using the term time.

There are numerous answers to an enormous number of time-related questions, from ancient philosophers to contemporary thinkers, from a biological standpoint to a physical one, and from reserved explanations to intricate ones. This brief note shares my attempt to grasp the concept of time by exploring a simple approach that resonates with me. My goal is not merely to define time or devise a mechanical measure for it. That would serve only as the first step toward addressing some perplexing questions, like, 'If time is a self-standing existence, how is it possible to perceive it subjectively?', 'How do we experience time passing at different paces throughout different stages of life?', and ultimately, 'What was there before the inception of the world?'[1]

A HYPOTHETICAL WORLD

Consider a two-dimensional world with no boundaries, exclusively hosting five entities: (1) emitter ✳, (2) reflector ◯, (3) absorbent, (4) white particle, and (5) black particle ▶. The following lists the definitions and assumptions in this world.

1. All entities have a zero-dimension and take up no space.[2]

2. All entities are massless.

3. The entities do not comprise any elemental components, such as atoms or subatomic particles.

4. Absorbents eliminate any particles if placed in the same position in space.

---

[1] I addressed these time perception issues in the appendix to this chapter; see page 65.

[2] Although all entities are 0-dimension dots, I inevitably draw them with visible symbols in the figures of this chapter.

5. Emitters continually generate and emit white particles[3] in every possible direction.

6. White particles are inert and show no interaction with any entity, except for absorbents.

7. All entities can detect the presence of white particles without imposing any changes in their trajectory.

8. Reflectors can generate and release labeled black particles at will and identify them if they return.

9. If a black particle hits a reflector, the particle instantaneously experiences an alteration in its trajectory by 180 degrees.

10. All particles travel at the same constant speed with no possibility of accelerating.

In the following, I utilize these assumptions to explore the concept of time. There may be instances where I depict a particle's path as a straight line, which assumes a hypothetical scenario where all objects are massless (thus no gravity) and situated in a static setup (thus no acceleration). Nevertheless, these straight lines serve as conceptual aids, while the particles' actual directions do not impact the discussion. The core idea is that if two particles are placed in the same spatial position to move in the same direction, they traverse identical trajectories with the same speed.

---

[3] In this chapter, I may refer to white particles as the *images of the emitter*.

STAND-STILL WORLDS

Consider a world consisting of two reflectors A and B, as illustrated in **Figure 9**.

Figure 9 | A world comprising two reflectors.

From A's perspective, the world appears empty as it lacks the capability to perceive the presence of B. Despite our vantage point encompassing both A and B, none of them can discern the other's existence because detection relies on particle travel between observers, a phenomenon absent in this hypothetical scenario. In this world, the concept of time is meaningless.

One may ask, 'Does this imply that if I remain motionless, time loses its relevance, rendering my world timeless?' My response is, 'No matter how motionless you stand, physiological functions like breathing and heartbeats persist; these movements do not align with the stationary nature of the world sketched in this scenario. Furthermore, if all movement ceases, including the flow of electromagnetic radiation from the Sun (sunlight), our world may resemble the hypothetical scenario described here; however, we would no longer be alive to experience such a timeless world.'

WORLDS WITH MOVING OBJECTS

The world we live in is not filled with stand-still objects but with moving ones. So, we will continue this study by exploring such worlds with moving objects.

Consider a scenario in which A releases a black particle that is by chance toward B, as illustrated in **Figure 10**. This specific direction results in a reflection of that black particle, which makes it return to A, allowing A to identify the existence of a reflector (B) in the world.

Figure 10 | A world with two reflectors, A and B, where A release a black particle along a direction toward B, indicated by the dotted line.

When A releases the black particle, the particle travels with a constant velocity toward B. Upon hitting B, the particle reflects back toward A along the same trajectory. A promptly identifies the returned particle. From A's perspective, it releases a particle at one instant (denoted as I0) and detects its presence at another instant (denoted as I1), and A experiences no other intervening events between these two, meaning that there is no other instant between I0 and I1 for A. In other words, A releases the particle at I0 and instantly detects its return at I1. This observation holds true regardless of how many times A repeats the experiment.

A question may arise: 'How long does it take for the particle to travel from A to B and back?' My response echoes what I just mentioned: 'No time.' This statement may appear counterintuitive, given our everyday experiences where any movement involves a measurable duration. Considering the particles travel with a constant speed under any condition and there is a non-zero distance between A and B, some time must elapse for the particle to complete its round trip between the two reflectors. This apparent contradiction arises from the fact that the speed of the particles is not pre-assigned. Consequently, in the current scenario, the particle travels at an immeasurable speed.

Let us continue our exploration by adjusting the world's design to establish a framework for measuring time, rendering assumption 10, which mandates a constant speed for all particles, relevant. To achieve this, we straightforwardly introduce a reference by adding an emitter $\mathcal{E}$, which from A's point of view, consistently moves along a straight line and oscillates between two points in the space. **Figure 11** illustrates such a world.

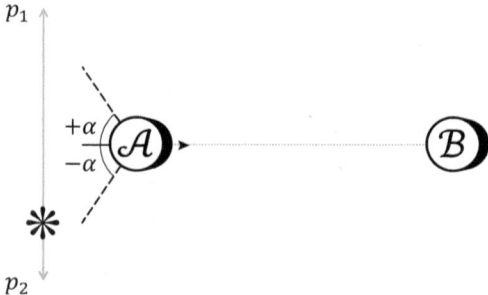

Figure 11 | A world with two reflectors, A and B, and a moving emitter $\mathcal{E}$ that oscillates between p_1 and p_2, two arbitrary points on the space. Measuring $\mathcal{E}$'s position by a deviation angle θ with respect to the line connecting the centers of A and B (indicated by the dotted line), the emitter oscillates between $+\alpha$ (at p_1) and $-\alpha$ (at p_2).

Defining DAY and HAND

In the coming sections for studying the world depicted in **Figure II**, we need to measure time and distance. For that, I use 'DAY' as the unit of time and 'HAND' as the unit of length. Here are the definitions of these two units:

- 1 HAND is the distance between $\mathcal{A}$ and $\mathcal{B}$.

- 1 DAY is the time period during which $\mathcal{A}$ observes $\mathcal{E}$ traveling a full oscillation, which can be marked if the absolute changes in the deviation angle are $|\Delta\theta| = 4\alpha$. For example, $\mathcal{E}$ travelling $p_1 \to p_2 \to p_1$ marks a full oscillation.

Perception of time for a stationary observer

Consider the world described in **Figure II**, where from the instant $\mathcal{A}$ releases a particle toward $\mathcal{B}$ (I0) until it detects the particle's return (I1), $\mathcal{A}$ observes another phenomenon: the change in $\mathcal{E}$'s position. Let us assume $\mathcal{A}$ releases the particle when $\mathcal{E}$ is at p_1. From that instant until I1, $\mathcal{A}$ observes $\mathcal{E}$ traveling a path with $\theta = 0 \to +\alpha \to -\alpha \to +\alpha \to -\alpha \to 0$;[4] meaning that $\mathcal{A}$ perceives it takes 2 DAYs between I0 and I1.

Perception of time for a moving observer

Continuing with nearly the same scenario, let us explore the particle's perception of time. The adjustment I am introducing to

---

[4] A travel of $p_1 \to p_2$, which changes the deviation angle as $+\alpha \to -\alpha$, results in $|\Delta\theta| = 2\alpha$.

maintain simplicity is that A releases the particle upon observing $\mathcal{E}$ positioned at $\theta = 0$, that is, along the line connecting the centers of A and B.[5]

Consider the particle observes $\mathcal{E}$ at $\theta = 0$, marking I0 when A releases it toward B. Both the black particle and the image of $\mathcal{E}$ (the white particle arrived from $\mathcal{E}$, marking its position at $\theta = 0$ from A's and the black particle's perspectives) move along the same path and at the same constant speed. Consequently, the black particle exclusively observes the image of $\mathcal{E}$ at $\theta = 0$ as an unchanging entity for the path of $A \rightarrow B$. This implies that for this part of the journey, the black particle observes no change in the reference to bringing time into existence.

At the end of this part of the trip and upon hitting B, the black particle instantly takes the opposite direction, while the companion white particle passes through B. Thus far, the black particle has experienced two instants of I0 (leaving A) and IB (reaching B) with no passage of time between them. Now, as the black particle travels back towards A, it views the white particles of $\mathcal{E}$ passing through its trajectory, observing the emitter moving a path as $\theta = 0 \rightarrow +\alpha \rightarrow -\alpha \rightarrow +\alpha \rightarrow -\alpha \rightarrow 0$, covering 2 DAYS. Subsequently, the black particle returns to A, marking the instant I1.

COMPARING THE OBSERVED TIMELINES

Let us explore the scenarios outlined and compare the perception of time between two observers: A and the black particle. When we observe this hypothetical world from a different angle, the simultaneous movements of the particle and the emitter make us perceive time in the same way as observer A, but not from the black

---

[5]Once A observes $\mathcal{E}$ at any position, $\mathcal{E}$ has already moved along its defined path.

On Time

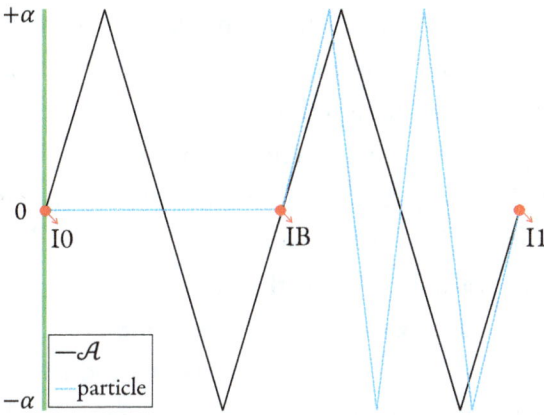

Figure 12 | Comparison between the time perceived by the stationary observer ($\mathcal{A}$) and the moving observer (black particle). $\mathcal{A}$ marks I0 when $\mathcal{E}$ is at $\theta = 0$, observing the movement of $\mathcal{E}$ as shown in the graph until it detects the particle's return and marks I1. Similarly, the particle marks I0 when $\mathcal{E}$ is at $\theta = 0$, and, without experiencing any changes, it marks IB. From then, it observes the movements of $\mathcal{E}$ as shown in the graph until it reaches $\mathcal{A}$ and marks I1.

particle's viewpoint. To understand how the particle perceives time, a graph, like the one depicted in **Figure 12**, becomes a useful tool.

According to these observations summarized in **Figure 12**, $\mathcal{A}$ concludes that it takes two DAYS for the black particle to depart from $\mathcal{A}$, reach $\mathcal{B}$, and return. To calculate the speed of the particle, we require a unit of length for which we use HAND. Thus, from $\mathcal{A}$'s viewpoint, the particle moves at a speed of '2 HANDS per 2 DAYS'. While it is tempting to simplify this fraction to '1 HAND per 1 DAY', it is crucial to note that, at least in the depicted setup in **Figure 12**, $\mathcal{A}$ lacks the means to confirm that the black particle moves 1 HAND in 1 DAY. $\mathcal{A}$'s instruments are bound to $\mathcal{A}$, with no access to collect data from $\mathcal{B}$. Therefore, although this simplification is mathematically supported ($2/2 = 1$), its physical meaning cannot be justified experimentally. Nevertheless, in this thought experiment, the simplification can be justified based on assumption 10, expressing that all particles always move with a constant speed.

Now, let us examine the particle's perception of time. Would it be the same as $\mathcal{A}$'s? The particle observes I0 and IB next to each other without any time interval between them. Then, it moves toward $\mathcal{A}$ and observes two DAYs from the movement of $\mathcal{E}$ until it marks I1. This suggests that, from the particle's viewpoint, it moves with an immeasurable speed from $\mathcal{A}$ to $\mathcal{B}$, and with a speed of '2 HAND per 1 DAY' from $\mathcal{B}$ to $\mathcal{A}$. In short, $\mathcal{A}$ and the black particle hold two distinct (para-) opinions (doxa) about the particle's speed.

One may ask, 'Why does the black particle observe nothing between I0 and IB? Should it not witness the white particles emitted by $\mathcal{E}$ passing through its path, similar to its return journey?' Considering that the black particle begins its journey when observing $\mathcal{E}$ at $\theta = 0$, all previously emitted white particles of $\mathcal{E}$ are ahead of the black particle. Since all particles move at the exact same speed, the black particle never overtakes any of those previously emitted white particles of $\mathcal{E}$ during its journey from $\mathcal{A}$ to $\mathcal{B}$.

Conclusions

The following can be deduced from our examinations:

- Time begins to exist for an observer only when an observable moving reference exists.

- The perception of time depends on the observer.

- Time and instant are two separate concepts that cannot be merged. A reference is necessary to introduce the concept of time into existence, while the concept of instant can exist independently.

THE WORLD BEFORE CREATION

One's accepted viewpoint about being hints at the direction to approach the question of the world before creation. For those advocating the primacy of the mind, a plausible answer could be, 'There was what there was!' A more assured answer is, 'Nothing. The (master)mind came into existence first, and then it created the world.' However, proponents of the mind's primacy may not accept the second answer, claiming that 'The (master)mind necessarily existed before and will persist beyond the physical world.' This viewpoint aligns closely with how M3 conceives of time: timeless and eternal.

The other idea comes from the concept of the body's primacy, where time can be defined as described in this chapter: it exists only when an observer establishes a time reference, and accordingly, the perception of time is observer-dependent. Because the time reference requires, at the very least, the existence of physical bodies, it follows that there was no time before the physical world's creation due to the absence of any such reference. Furthermore, it implies an origin for time coinciding with the inception of the physical world, particularly in a setup where time can be established.[6]

---

[6]This bodily view of time also allows us to explain personal perceptions of time changing through different stages of life; see further discussions on page 65.

On Time—*Further discussions*

The concept of time routinely appears in various forms and notions throughout our lives. We often rely on standardized community-accepted units of time, like seconds, hours, and days, for practical purposes such as scheduling meetings. However, beyond these mechanically tracked measures, our perception of time varies across different life stages and circumstances. These personal and subjective perceptions of time may lead a person to disbelieve the existence of time as a physically meaningful phenomenon. Regardless of such a belief, the impact of time on us is undeniable. This appendix explores *'our perception of time'* and different *'confusions in the perceived time'*.

The last section of this appendix explores *'the possibility of backward time travel'*. While this topic does not contribute to the questions I pursued in other sections, this subject is interesting, particularly because, from a physics standpoint, there exists no inherent arrow of time.

Our perception of time

Since the perception of time depends on the observer, each observer must select a reference and link it with an available memory unit to establish the concept of time and make it useful. This implies that an animal of BL0 or BL1 lacks the capacity to grasp the concept of time. A BL2 animal, equipped with M1, can take advantage of a changing phenomenon as a reference for gauging time. One of the simplest changing phenomena is appetite: when the animal becomes hungry, and its memory unit marks that event as the starting point to search for food.

Furthermore, BL2 animals may also take advantage of alternating external events, not necessarily to establish a time measurement unit but to become in sync with those events. For example, if a BL2 animal finds food in time intervals close to its eating cycles in a different location from its usual habitat, the animal's trained M1 links the two events and instructs it to seek food at expected time intervals.

This implies that time does not necessarily need to be defined based on an external phenomenon; however, an external-based reference helps to define time less subjectively. Animals with a trained M1 can observe the behavior of different body parts and use them as time markers. Moreover, these animals can accurately sync their internal time tracker with external events, such as waking and sleeping with the daylight cycle.

The same principle applies when BL3 or BL4 animals solely rely on their M1 for actions. For instance, a pianist playing a well-practiced piece relies on the trained memory of her muscles to hit the notes at precise timing. If she involves her M2 or M3 units during the performance, reflecting her momentary emotions, some changes may be observed, whether subtle when played solo

On Time—Further discussions

or noticeable when played with others.

The memory units M2 and M3 grant animals the ability to imagine, enabling them to establish time measures that can be communicated through language.

As I explained earlier, BL3 animals can construct the measure of time using external events. Living on Earth allows them to experience recurring events like the Sun's movement in the sky, day and night cycles, and seasonal changes, all of which serve as reliable markers for measuring time. Some behaviors may be instinctual, implanted into the PN unit. These animals can also use externally available changing phenomena as the base to measure time, communicate their perceived time with each other using their primary language, and cooperate in planned activities.

For instance, if the mission is a hunt, timing may be co-ordinated around the prey's water-drinking habits, prompting the whole tribe of predators to attack for food, regardless of individual hunger levels.

This capacity of a trained M2 is what humans mostly use to keep track of time: establishing a time measurement unit based on externally observable events that can be communicated with others. Currently, the widely accepted measurement unit of time is the second, defined by the fixed numerical value of the caesium frequency.[1]

Referring back to the initial statement in this section, we must clarify how the memory units contribute to our perception of time, beyond their role in timekeeping.

---

[1] A second is defined as the time interval during which the unperturbed ground-state hyperfine transition frequency of the caesium-133 atom is 9,192,631,770.

Each memory unit operates differently in handling stored information. Those stored in M1 essentially function when called upon, and since M1 is unable to make imaginations, its stored information is not to be recalled out of action. This implies that these memories are entirely out of reach in stationary situations.

Parallel to that, M3 stores information without any inherent time frame, as it deals with abstract and imagination-based imaginations, which are essentially timeless. Consequently, M3 treats all its stored memories as timeless entities, devoid of any temporal context.

One might argue that even imagination-based imaginations are time-bound; for example, imagining chatting with an alien over dinner presumably takes time. My answer is that M3 would trigger M2 to aid with its physical-based imagination power. In this scenario, the setup (which would be fantasized uniquely by each individual) is imagined by the stimulated M2, while the concept of conversing with an extraterrestrial over dinner, originating in M3, remains formless and timeless.

This brings us to the memory unit M2, which is crucial for synchronizing M1's and, more importantly, M3's information with external events for timekeeping purposes. M2, responsible for physical imagination, uses its stored information and imagination for further training to enhance its performance or update its control unit. To achieve this, M2 must remember any detected sequence of events, at least those relevant to its function. This way, M2 shapes our perception of time within the physical realm by linking internal processes with external events.

CONFUSIONS IN THE PERCEIVED TIME

While we often rely on clocks to manage our activities, it is common to perceive short periods as extended or feel that distant memories are recent, and vice versa. I categorize these experiences as confusions in the perceived time, identifying two types of them: short-term and long-term.

SHORT-TERM CONFUSIONS

The disruption of an established, physical-based time measurement can disorient animals with BLs of 2, 3, and 4. In these animals, the PN unit is responsible for regulating different body parts irrespective of memory units. If PN syncs specific tasks with certain external events (effectively using those events as a time measurement), the animal may struggle with those tasks when its PN becomes confused. For instance, if an animal accustomed to sleeping in darkness is suddenly placed in a perpetually bright space, it might experience sleep problems. While a BL2 animal may initially suffer, its PN can adapt relatively quickly. However, a BL3 animal takes more time to adapt because its imagination-based expectations keep the brain active for longer, providing less time for adaptation and hindering the process. Eventually, through repeated experiences and memory formation, the animal can adapt to the new situation, that is, sleeping in the bright environment.

The process for a BL4 animal may differ significantly, as its M3 can override other instructions. In our scenario, a BL4 animal may resist the new bright situation. Conversely, its M3 may persuade its M2 to cease imagination and adapt swiftly—an approach akin to embracing the present moment and surrendering to life.

Another form of confusion can occur when the constructed time measures of various memory units receive mismatched time-dependent information.

Consider a BL2 animal, generally secure in following its constructed time. While its M1 can accurately act based on tracked events, any not-yet-learned physical change, such as weakness caused by an injury, can lead to mistimed actions with its possible physical consequences. For instance, if an animal needs to catch food using a specific technique but fails due to mistimed actions caused by weakness, it may face starvation.

The situation differs for BL3 and BL4 animals, capable of reconstructing and re-evaluating imaginations and their corresponding controlled decisions, which allow for timely expectations of imaginary events. If the measured time for an event contradicts expectations, confusion can arise from the imagination of potential events. In some cases, the animal's M2 may use the updated information to devise new plans. However, not all situations require or permit planning, and confusion may cause a BL3 animal to perceive objectively equal durations differently: a happy day may seem to end in a blink, while an idle day may feel endless.

This illustrates that short-term time perception is linked to local time references, primarily from M2's perspective. Training M1 directly involves physical actions, such as building muscle memory, synchronized with physically available time references sensed without distortion. However, for M2, local time references can be distorted due to its imagined expectations.

Let me elucidate this with three scenarios in which $\mathcal{A}$, an animal with a BL of 3 or 4, undergoes a recurring event V bounded between two instances, I0 and I1, lasting only for one DAY. There are only

On Time—Further discussions

two possible states regarding V: being either IN or OUT of it. All scenarios begin with A being IN V.[2]

1. A is IN V. It has no predetermined preference regarding staying IN or going OUT of V and can freely transition between these states. After remaining IN V for a while, A decides to go OUT of V, and it does so. Later, A chooses to return to being IN V. This back-and-forth movement between states may occur multiple times until the end of the DAY, marked by I1, when V ends.

    In this accustomed life, A does not perceive time passing strangely, as the experience aligns with its established time reference. Additionally, since A can change its states at will, it may not view V as painful. A marks this DAY as an ordinary one.

2. A is IN V. It prefers to be OUT of V but must remain IN V. So, A stays IN V while its M2 consistently envisions A being OUT of V, realizing it is still IN V. This loop continues until V ends at I1.

    These rapid changes between M2's imagination and realization cause A to pseudo-experience the change with a higher frequency than its accustomed rate depicted in scenario 1. A higher frequency does not mean M2 perceives time passing faster; it is exactly the opposite. M2 is accustomed to experiencing changes between IN and OUT only a few times during one DAY. Increasing the number of the changes—that is, increasing the frequency of the internal time reference—confuses M2, as it anticipates I1 only after

---

[2] To put into picture, imagine V as a workday with I0 and I1 marking its start and end, respectively. IN corresponds to actual work, while OUT denotes breaks.

the first couple of changes in the states. If I1 does not occur by then—as in this scenario—M2 undergoes a lengthening of the duration between I0 and I1, inconsistent with its memories and perhaps objective time references like a clock or the natural light cycle.

In short, an animal with a trained M2, expecting no change in its state of being, experiences a temporal extension if it pseudo-experiences high-frequency events, potentially leading to fatigue, stress, or frustration. A marks this DAY as a long one.

3. A is IN V. It prefers to stay IN V and remains IN V until I1.

The local time reference is again different from what A is accustomed to, but this time, unlike scenario 2, the frequency is much lower. In fact, if A stays IN V for the duration between I0 and I1, it experiences no changes in its state, causing A's M2 to perceive a shorter duration between these two states than in scenario 1. A marks this DAY as a short one.

Lastly, let me add a note about experiencing a stop in the passing of time, exclusively possible for BL4 animals when their M3 is in action. Since M3 lacks a time reference, if an action is fundamentally M3-driven, the animal does not perceive the passing of time. As an example, consider a master painter who begins a painting in her solitude and a well-equipped studio. The master works with the chosen medium with ease and employs any technique she needs with confidence, all from her memory. For her, the only task is to keep imagining the parts of the scene she is working on, which is the responsibility of M3. The master may continue painting until

On Time—Further discussions

she is interrupted by a physical cause, such as an alarm to stretch, becoming hungry, or a need to use the toilet.

LONG-TERM CONFUSIONS

While animals with a BL of 0 and 1 require performing numerous bodily functions, they are not obligated to keep their tasks time-dependent. Animals equipped with memory units, however, can benefit from tracking time. As a survival strategy, animals often live according to their established time measures, linking time to identifiable signs, whether internal (such as hunger) or external (such as a traffic light turning green). This strategy proves effective for short-term needs. However, understanding longer durations necessitates the ability to imagine events. In these cases, accumulated (pseudo-)experienced memories in M2 shape the animal's perception of time.[3]

Depending on the functionality of the M2-dedicated cells, memories may remain intact or become distorted over time. Some details might become disordered, overwritten by other memories, lost by the death of the memory cells, or altered by other M2- or M3-based imaginations. The latter is when M2 takes one of its imaginations (regardless of the stimulating origin) as a real memory, mistaking it for a physically experienced event. This can directly impact M2's imagination of M1-based abilities, potentially benefiting or harming the animal.

While for short-term tracking, M2 compares various signals to align internal and external signs, for long-term tracking, it may

---

[3] In the last paragraphs of the section 'our perception of time' on page 67, I explained that M1 and M3 possess timeless information, while only M2 is responsible for imagining traceable time that can be shared through language.

lose specific time references and instead rely on sequencing events. If prompted, it reconstructs a sense of time by recalling time-dependent elements available from that sequence or fabricating them using its power of imagination. It would try to mark time as accurately as it can and may not be successful on many occasions. This implies that the memories may be felt out of time. Some memories may feel recent, but upon comparison with external references like calendars, they reveal themselves as experienced long ago. This discrepancy can be attributed to the significant effort and time invested in processing those memories, which played a crucial role in training M2, thus making them vividly remembered. As the animal ages, the new memories play increasingly less influential roles in M2's development, causing them to be perceived as more distant.

However, this does not necessarily imply that an animal with a trained M2 stops with training this unit. It may continue to do so, but its M2 (and M3, if available) often fall back on established patterns of imagination. This reliance on accumulated memories rather than exploration of new methods speeds up task performance and aligns with the animal's expectations. Consequently, the animal perceives life as progressing with a lower frequency of impactful events than during training times. As a result, stored instances seem closer together, creating the impression of a shorter timeline or a faster-paced life as the animal ages.

On Time—Further discussions

THE POSSIBILITY OF BACKWARD TIME TRAVEL

Let us explore a couple of hypothetical scenarios and examine the costs of backward time travel. The timeline depicted in **Figure 12** spans only two DAYs, bounded by the two instants I0 and I1. To initiate a journey back from I1 to I0, consider abruptly reversing the movement direction of $\mathcal{E}$ and releasing the particle to travel towards $\mathcal{B}$. Without altering anything else, the perception of time for both $\mathcal{A}$ and the particle unfolds as illustrated in **Figure 13**.

Figure 13 suggests that observer $\mathcal{A}$ observes a reversal in the movement of $\mathcal{E}$ between the instants I1 and I0, which can be interpreted as backward time travel. The crucial point, however, is the particle's perception of time, which does not mirror the past. Instead, it jumps from instant I1 to IB and only then begins

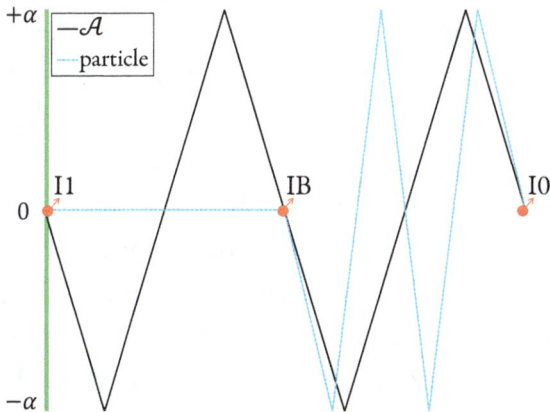

Figure 13 | Comparison between the time perceived by $\mathcal{A}$ and the black particle. This graph can be considered a continuation of **Figure 12**, where the emitter's movement is suddenly reversed and the particle is released at $\theta = 0$.

perceiving time as it travels back towards $\mathcal{A}$ to mark I0, observing the reverse movement of $\mathcal{E}$.

But why does not the particle observe everything in reverse? The reason lies in two other changes not imposed on this reversed world: reversing the moving direction of $\mathcal{E}$'s emitted white particles and converting $\mathcal{E}$ from an emitter to an absorbent. If we only reverse the direction of $\mathcal{E}$'s movement and allow it to emit white particles as before, the black particle observes instants I1 and IB adjacent, witnessing $\mathcal{E}$'s movement only along its return path to $\mathcal{A}$, unless these other two changes are imposed. Only then does the black particle also observe reverse time travel.

By converting the emitter to an absorbent and redirecting all previously emitted white particles to it, this world not only appears but actually undergoes a reverse timeline.[4]

So, the possibility of traveling backward in time presents a nuanced answer—it is both yes and no, dependent on the scale of the event in question. If a subject can transition from one state to a previous one, experiencing everything in reverse order, then that subject undergoes backward time travel. However, the likelihood of such an event occurring is a fundamentally different question.

In our example, $\mathcal{A}$ experiences backward time travel once $\mathcal{E}$ moves in reverse, whether it remains an emitter or becomes an absorbent, while the particle's experience differs. This suggests that for the entire world to go back in time, every single thing must move backward along the exact path it took during its forward progression, unless different paths are indistinguishable.

To demonstrate the significance of the path-dependency in

---

[4] If an animal undergoes backward time travel, it loses its memory of it.

On Time—Further discussions

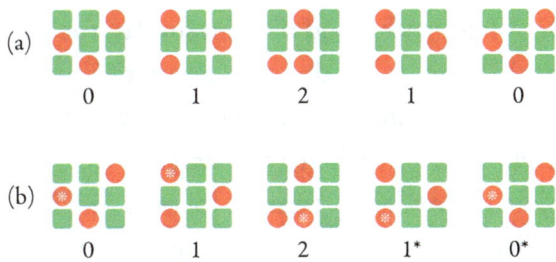

Figure 14 | 5 instants of 9 particles (3 red circles and 6 green squares) arranged in an initial order marked as 0. The particles' orders are captured at other instants as well. The difference between (a) and (b) is that the red circles are non-differentiable in (a), while one of them is marked in (b) to track its position.

time travel, consider the following setup in which the 9 particles illustrated in **Figure 14** are initially arranged as in state 0.

The particles can be rearranged in any order, and whenever they change positions, a snapshot of their order is captured. Let us assume the state of this group of particles changes as 0→1→2. Then, the group experiences a change of states as 2→1→0. Can we then conclude that this group of particles moved back in time?

To begin with, time does not exist in this hypothetical world, as we have not yet defined an observable moving reference, and without it, we are dealing with a sequence of instances rather than a temporal progression. If we introduce an observable moving reference that moves in reverse along with the reverse alterations in the group's order, only then can we assess whether the group has experienced backward time travel.

Suppose there is a reference, showing a backward movement when the group reorders as 2→1→0. In case (a) of **Figure 14**, it appears that backward time travel occurs. But does the same apply to case (b)? While states 0 and 0* seem similar, the marked circle reveals that the path 2→0* does not accurately mirror the path 0→2 because state 1* differs from 1. This discrepancy indicates that although events at a scale where the marked circle is indistinguishable may seem reversed, they actually follow a different trajectory. This contradicts the essence of backward time travel, which involves moving backward along a previously traveled path.

Quick reference

This chapter provides very brief descriptions of several terms mentioned in the book.

Müller-Lyer illusion

In 1889, Franz Carl Müller-Lyer introduced an optical illusion involving three arrowheads, as depicted in **Figure 15**. When individuals are prompted to indicate the central point of the line, they often position the marker closer to the arrowhead that points outward.

You can interactively try to spot the mid-point of this arrow on Dr. Michael Bach's website at:
 https://michaelbach.de/ot/sze-muelue.

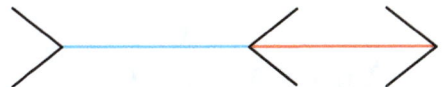

Figure 15 | Müller-Lyer illusion. The line segments on the left (blue) and right (red) are of equal length.

Ponzo illusion

The Ponzo illusion, popularized by Mario Ponzo in 1911, involves illustrating two equal-length lines within a set of diverging lines, as depicted in **Figure 16**. Despite being the same size, the parallel lines appear to be of varying lengths.

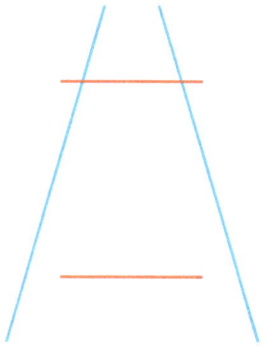

Figure 16 | Ponzo illusion. The parallel line segments (red) are of equal length.

McGurk effect

In 1976, an auditory illusion was described by Harry McGurk and John MacDonald. This phenomenon arises when the sound one hears is combined with a visual from a different source, resulting in the perception of a distinct third sound.

Shepard tone

The Shepard tone, named after Roger Shepard from his 1964 publication, is made up of overlapping sine waves that are an octave apart. When this tone's lowest note shifts up or down, it is called the Shepard scale. This effect produces the auditory illusion of a tone that seems to endlessly rise or fall in pitch despite getting actually no higher or lower.

Thermal grill illusion

In 1896, Torsten Thunberg first showcased the thermal grill tactile illusion, which is produced by a grill consisting of alternating bars at warm (for example, 40°C or 104°F) and cold (for instance, 20°C or 68°F) temperatures. Although touching the individual bars feels relatively comfortable, when someone presses their hand against the entire grill, they experience a deceptive sensation of burning heat.

Sphinx

A sphinx is a mythical creature with the head of a human, the body of a lion, and the wings of an eagle. This creature appears in both Egyptian and Greek mythology. The largest and most renowned sphinx is the Great Sphinx of Giza, located on the Giza Plateau near the Great Pyramids of Giza.

Similar hybrid creatures have been discovered in various cultures. For instance, the 32,000-years-old Löwenmensch figurine was found in the Hohlenstein-Stadel cave in Germany. Another example is Mard-xār (meaning "man-eater") from Persian mythology, which is more commonly referred to by its translated name, the Manticore.

Lamassu

Lamassu is a creature from ancient Mesopotamian mythology. It was portrayed as a hybrid of a human, a bird, and either a bull or a lion. This creature is characterized by a human face, the body of a bull or lion, and the wings of a bird. Notable instances of Lamassu can be found at the Gate of All Nations in Persepolis, Iran.

www.ingramcontent.com/pod-product-compliance
Lightning Source LLC
Chambersburg PA
CBHW070313010526
44107CB00004B/332